PENNY STOCKS
FOR BEGINNERS

HOW TO GET RICH
INVESTING IN PENNY STOCKS

ClydeBank Media LLC
P.O Box 6561
Albany, NY 12206
Printed in the United States of America

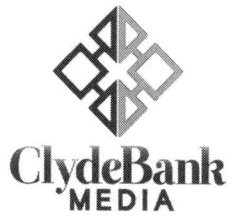

Copyright © 2015
ClydeBank Media LLC
www.clydebankmedia.com
All Rights Reserved

ISBN-13 : 978-1499522358

CONTENTS

INTRODUCTION

Before we dive into the book, we want to let you in on a secret.

Are you ready?

There is no such thing as a legitimate "get rich quick" system.

Believe me, I have tried nearly every method online and off, to "get rich overnight" and none of them work. Anyone who has told you that they made their fortunes overnight or by not working hard is flat out lying. So, why am I telling you this? Isn't this a book on how to "get rich?" The fact of the matter is that acquiring wealth is a long process that requires a lot hard work and most importantly, knowledge. I am not saying there are not proven methods that will allow you to obtain financial freedom in your life; because there are, and Penny Stock Investing is one of them.

There are many ways to develop wealth without slaving away at a 9-5 job you loathe; however, to successfully implement these methods you need to have the knowledge, the drive and the will to succeed. I cannot instill within you a thirst for more, a desire to live the life you have always dreamed of for yourself, a determination that will not be shattered no matter what obstacles you face. What I can provide you with, however, is the knowledge and strategies to turn that passion into a functional reality.

The goal of this book is to give you the necessary knowledge and strategies to successfully invest in Penny Stocks, thus providing endless wealth and the ability to enjoy the finest things this world has to offer. The steps are there, the advice is clear; the money is on the table. All you need to do is read this book, follow the guidance provided and implement the strategies.

Welcome to the first day of the rest of your life.

CHAPTER ONE
The Stock Exchange

Penny stocks were created for the small investor. As the word implies, penny stocks are stocks with a share value of $1 or less. The Securities and Exchange Commission (SEC) later modified this definition to include all shares with a value of less than $5.00. What you need to understand is that penny stocks were created for a specific purpose - they were designed to attract small investors. These stocks are perfect for people who want to invest in stocks but do not have the resources to match the big players.

Why would one want to invest in penny stocks? Well, the answer is simple. People want to make money and they see an opportunity in the stock market. This is possibly one of the easiest ways to earn a decent income However, you got to be savvy enough to do so, since it is easier said than done. Since penny stocks were the result of trading on the stock exchanges, their existence came about quite naturally. It was a gradual process of transition rather than one of sustained action. In other words, those who created these stocks did not intentionally design them for profit generation for the investors. They came to be called penny stocks because the companies of these stocks were too small to be listed on the stock exchanges. Today no one bothers about these companies and no one gives them a second thought, except, of course, those who wish to trade the shares of such companies.

The Stock Exchange

Trading penny stocks is radically different, as most of them are not listed on the major stock exchanges such as NASDAQ and the Dow Jones. Almost all countries have their own "penny stock" companies. The European stock exchanges such as the London FTSE and the German Xetra Dax also do not list the penny stock companies. So, the obvious question that one is tempted to ask is, how do you trade shares of companies that are not officially listed on the stock exchange? The answer is quite simple: pink sheets and OTCBB. These penny stocks can be found on what are called 'Pink Sheets' and OTCBB or 'Over The Counter Bulletin Boards'. Stocks that are listed on the "Pink Sheets" typically end with the suffix ".PK" and this shows that this particular stock is traded over the counter or OTC. This may come as a surprise to you because these stocks got their names from the original piece of pink paper on which they were printed. This is how the term 'pink sheets' became widely used in investment circles. These companies are not required to submit information to the Securities Exchange Commission or the SEC. They are not even required to maintain certain minimum requirements for trading. The National Quotation Bureau provides the 'bid and ask prices' every day for such stocks. This bureau was first set up in 1913 to list and monitor such stocks. In 1999, the National Quotation Bureau started the real-time electronic price quotation system and thus began the era of computerized trading for penny stocks.

Today about 15,000 stocks trade on the pink sheets. This is a huge number to choose from and add to that the fact that most of these have low bid and ask prices. You must exercise caution as not much can be garnered about the performance of these stocks. For some reason, these companies prefer not to be listed on the major stock exchanges of the world. This fact should be borne in mind always. Do not be taken in by the lure of quick profits. You must also remember that many of these companies listed on the pink sheets are there due to poor performance. Some of them have been delisted for various reasons, while some of these stocks have fallen below the $1 mark and hence they are traded on the pink sheets. All these facts must be taken into consideration as well. Sometimes the cost of being listed on the major stock exchanges is unbearable for some of these companies. They seek a short inexpensive route to being traded publicly. They are there to make a quick buck at the expense of the small investor. Getting listed on say, the NASDAQ or the Dow Jones would entail these companies to file the necessary paperwork and provide all sorts of information. Some of these companies want to bypass this process. This is especially true for foreign companies that are based offshore. They would need expert legal help to get listed on the top stock exchanges of the world. Hiring top legal aid is always an expensive affair.

Do you know what Volkswagen, Nestle, and Nintendo have in common? Pink sheets! Yes, pink sheets! All these very highly reputable companies are listed on the pink sheets as well. For these companies, the same reasons apply as stated above although they are worth billions. Hence, it would be a smart move to invest in such reputable companies that trade on the pink sheets. But, there is a downside to it as well. The stocks of these companies do not go for under a dollar. They are highly valued and you need a considerable amount to invest in these companies. But if you have the money and are patient, these pink sheet stocks can be invaluable. Another negative aspect of the pink sheet stocks is that you cannot short sell. In other words, short selling and margins are not allowed. Sometimes, this can actually be a good thing as it can protect your investment. Moreover, it can also control your impulsive streak.

Finally, there are quite a few scam companies that are set up to defraud investors of their hard-earned money. These fraudulent companies are set up as offshore companies and then listed on the pink sheets. There is very little information about these companies as not much is mandatory. The shares of these companies are absolutely worthless. However, those who set up the company use all possible tools and loopholes to promote their company's shares. If you invest in such stocks, you might find one day that they'll just pull the rug from under your feet, leaving you wondering what hit you.

Despite all this, it is possible to make money with penny stocks. One just needs to be careful. The idea behind all this is to draw your attention to the dangers and pitfalls of trading in penny stocks so you can avoid them along the way. Once you are aware of how and where you can go wrong, you are prepared to do what is right and what is needed to make money by trading penny stocks from home. You can pick your stocks from the OTCBB and make money if you are smart enough and learn when and how to pick penny stocks. This is probably one reason why people are a bit wary of penny stocks. They are not listed on the major stock exchanges and this makes people suspicious.

Market Capitalization

The major stock exchanges of the world list large-cap, medium-cap, and micro-cap companies. These are listed in order of market capitalization. Large-cap companies such as Exxon have market capitalization worth billions of dollars. Similarly, Apple Inc. and Microsoft have market capitalization that exceeds the total GDP of some small countries. On the other end of the spectrum, there are the micro-cap companies. These companies have market capitalization that is worth a few million dollars only. In some cases, it could be even less. This is one reason why these companies are not listed on the stock exchange since they are too small to be listed. In other words, they are not fully capitalized and this makes such small companies especially vulnerable. Most small start-up companies are listed on Pink Sheets and OTCBB as they are yet to be listed as major companies on the official stock exchanges of the world. Sometimes very little is known about these companies. There is just not enough information available about them. You know nothing about the management of the company and you know nothing about its past performance. All this makes it very difficult to decide on the company's future. This is what scares many investors. For all these reasons, micro-cap or penny stock companies are always regarded with suspicion.

CHAPTER TWO

What Are Penny Stocks?

So, just what are penny stocks and why are they called so? Penny stocks are not what a big investor is going to be interested in. No one who has a large amount of capital and wants to invest in a stock is going to bother with penny stocks. If you look at the major stock exchanges, you will find hundreds or thousands of stocks listed. These are stocks of reputable companies. These stocks are often priced according to their market share and market capital. Most of the shares on the stock exchange are medium- to large-cap stocks. Their prices fluctuate but in all probability, the prices stay within a certain narrow band. Rarely do you see a company do so badly that it gets delisted. This is when it could be listed on the pink sheets and become a penny stock.

Take the example of BlackBerry. This Canadian company (formerly Research In Motion or RIM) has undergone a complete transformation. Just a few years ago, it was at the very top of its league, and now it has hit rock bottom. By last count, the shares of RIM were valued at about $4 and it could go down even further. According to new regulations, RIM should now be considered as a penny stock company. Would you invest in RIM? Would you be willing to take a chance and invest say $10,000 and buy say, 2500 shares of the company? This is where investor acumen comes into the picture. Who knows a few years down the road, the shares of RIM could climb back to over a hundred dollars and that would make you a very rich individual. Would you be willing to take that chance? This is what makes penny stocks so intriguing! You can buy these shares for a penny and hence the name for these shares. You will find these shares going for about $0.30 to $0.50 very often. These shares are transacted for less than a few dollars. This is the single biggest draw for most small investors. There is the lure for quick profits as well.

When a small investor thinks about investing in stocks, the first thing that comes to mind is the capital required to purchase a significant number of shares. Profits would be negligible without buying or selling a significant volume of shares. This is where penny stocks take center stage. Can you imagine how much it would take to buy about a thousand shares of Apple Inc. or Google! Apple Inc. shares are going at about $500 per shares and Google shares are at $1180 per share. Would you be able to afford that kind of money? You must also remember that there are millions of people willing to buy and sell penny stocks. If you take all these willing investors into consideration, the numbers quickly begin to make impressive reading.

There is an unfounded belief that penny stocks are really worthless.

Nothing could be further from the truth. There are many examples of penny stocks that have had their market value increase several hundred times over the course of a few years. You must remember that these are small-cap or micro-cap companies. This is why they are called penny stocks. Their market capitalization is just a few million dollars. This also makes them vulnerable to economic downturns like the one experienced in 2007-2008.

Penny stocks are also little known, as there is very little information available about them. Market regulations do not require them to reveal information, therefore there is very little that investors know about the companies. Since the shares of these companies are not well-regulated, they are open to increased manipulation. In fact, numerous cases have been filed against brokers and traders for fraudulent trading. All this makes trading in penny stocks a rather "iffy" affair.

In recent years, there has been a lot of hype about trading penny stocks. You see all kinds of adverts on television and radio about making it big with penny stocks. You may have even received emails about trading in penny stocks. All this is tempting and many investors believe what they see and hear about penny stocks. Unfortunately, not all of it is true. One has to be careful and filter the truth from the half-truths carefully. Before you embark on the risky venture of becoming a penny stock trader, it is essential you learn all you can about the fine art of buying and selling penny stocks. This could mean the difference between success and failure. It could also mean the difference between bankruptcy and solvency. You must remember that there is money to be made in trading penny stocks. There are numerous examples of people who have stuck to penny stocks and have ended up making a fortune. The key thing to remember is that there are huge possibilities. The opportunity exists. It is up to you to grab it with both hands and make the most of this incredible opportunity.

For those who want more out of life, this is an opportunity that you simply cannot afford to bypass. Such opportunities do not come again and again. However, it is easier said than done. Penny stocks are worth pennies but before you invest, you must remember that all trading is a risky business. If you are prepared to take a few risks, life is there for the taking. Nothing substantial and worthwhile can be gained without taking a few risks. The choice is yours. It is up to you to make well informed and educated choices when it comes to penny stocks. This is why you need to read on. This is one way to ensure that you never lose money with penny stocks.

CHAPTER THREE

History of Penny Stock Trading

Penny stocks have been traded for decades. However, it is only in recent times that penny stocks have come to the fore. Today, with computerized trading, penny stocks have become a source of great opportunities for traders. Computerized trading has made it possible to make substantial income through day trading penny stocks. There was a time when computerized trading was unknown and trading penny stocks was fraught with great risks. However, trading on computers has made it quite convenient to sell and buy penny stocks in a matter of seconds.

The entire process of buying and selling can be handled by you without any interference from your broker. This can make the entire process fast and efficient. You control everything all the time. This is why it is possible to make money within short periods of trading. To be able to trade penny stocks from the comfort of your home, all you need is a computer and a fast Internet connection. A broadband connection would be ideal. You will also need to be able to log in to a trading platform. In other words, you need access to a trading service. This trading service is often in the form of a trading platform that has all the bells and whistles for trading from home. Most online trading platforms are very good these days. You can buy and sell penny stocks very quickly at a click of the mouse. You will have to open a real trading account and deposit funds before you can start trading. You will have complete freedom to make your own decisions regarding the buying and selling of penny stocks. The prices you see on your screen are in real time. In nanoseconds, you can open and close a trade. You can book your profits whenever you want. You can cut your losses if things are going badly. You have complete control over every trade. Since 1999, fast electronic trading has revolutionized the trading markets. Millions of people now have access to the markets. In days of yore, only the banks and financial institutions were able to trade. There were a few private investors but they were few and far between. Computers and the Internet combined with online trading platforms have revolutionized the industry making it possible for millions of people to invest in stocks and earn money.

There are some people who believe that penny stocks go all the way to the days of the Great Depression. This is not entirely true. In those days, many companies traded below a dollar. This was because the value of the dollar was considerably greater. Incomes were lower and salaries were not what they are today. The rate of inflation is also much higher. Hence, penny stocks are really a recent phenomenon.

People have always evinced keen interest in the stock markets. A few savvy investors have even managed to make huge profits from investing in stocks. However, there is a saying going around the stock market – bulls make money, bears make money, only pigs get slaughtered. Here, the small investor often gets slaughtered. The big banks and financial institutions have large cash reserves and survive no matter what happens on the stock markets. For this reason, penny stocks have become especially attractive to small investors. Penny stocks allow small investors to compete with the big boys. This is why penny stocks have always drawn a lot of attention as they allow small investor to compete with large players in the field.

Penny stocks have been traded back in the seventies and early eighties as well. However, back then, the interest for penny stocks was not that great. Not many people viewed them as opportunities. These days, the story is entirely different. Penny stocks represent a great opportunity even if you do not have enough money to invest. Take the example of CANN or Advanced Cannabis Solution. The shares of this company were going at $3.25 recently. It is likely that the price of these shares will go well beyond $40 very quickly. This is a penny stock company that you could make a killing from. Cell Therapeutics Inc is a Seattle-based biotech company. It has great potential as most biotech companies are doing very well. This is also a penny stock company to watch out for. Another interesting prospect is Chelsea Therapeutics International Limited. This is yet another biotech penny stock company likely to do very well during the course of the coming years.

CHAPTER FOUR

Penny Stocks That Made People Millions

Penny stocks have allowed some savvy investors to make considerable amounts of money. Some penny stocks have grown from micro-stock companies to large-cap companies with many investors turned into millionaires overnight. However, it was not as sudden as one would like to think. In some cases, it took quite a few years for the shares to go beyond being worth just pennies. Most of the companies mentioned in this chapter went through turbulent times before emerging stronger. The turbulent times were the periods when the prices were practically at rock bottom. This was a good time to invest. Many people did and they were the ones who became millionaires a few years down the road.

If you have been thinking about investing in penny stocks look at these companies and their shares. Observe how their shares have grown in value over time. This is precisely what you should be wondering and dreaming about. This is how people make millions with penny stocks. You could be in their shoes too. Here are a few penny stocks that could have made you rich. Take the example of ***Pier 1 Imports***. This is one company whose shares sold for pennies bask in the late eighties and early nineties. Then gradually as the millennium approached, its share prices soared and it reached a record high of $25. Imagine what would have happened if you had bought ten thousand shares at $0.25 and then sold the lot at $25 per share. Yes, I know what you are thinking! A real windfall! Another one that made some people very happy was ***Concur Technologies***. You are going to be truly stunned by this one. In 2001, the shares of this company were trading at around $0.30 and now the price per share is a whopping $107. Yes, that right. You read that correctly, all this in about 13 years. If you were patient enough, you could have made millions.

Have you heard the story behind ***True Religion Apparel?*** This apparel company was going at 67 cents a share back in 2004. In just a few years, the share prices have skyrocketed to $32 per share. Look what happened to ***General Growth Properties***. This real estate company used to be in a financial mess and in 2009, it shares were selling at 59 cents. Now the price per share is a robust $21 and rising. There is yet another example of what can happen when you catch shares selling for a few pennies. Take the case of ***American Axle & Manufacturing***. The shares of this company hit rock bottom during the recent financial crisis. In 2009, the shares of this company stood at 40 cents. Today, these shares trade at more than $20 per share. What a windfall for those who managed to hang onto the shares of the company. There are innumerable examples of penny stocks that have been doing very well.

This is what penny stocks can do for you. All you have to do is be patient. Remember, when you buy at a few cents per share, your investment is always going to be small. If you are prepared to bid your time, you could experience a windfall sometime in the future.

It is all a game of patience.

CHAPTER FIVE
Managing Risks To Guarantee Rewards

Most people reading this book would have realized that while there are profits to be made in trading penny stocks one has to be very careful. There are rewards but there are significant risks as well. It is important to be aware of the risks. One has to be careful when trading penny stocks, as they are primarily micro-cap companies. The market share is low. Hence, many are unwilling to take a chance on them. Traders and especially the big banks and financial institutions are rarely interested in them. You will not find a great deal of interest being reported in the shares of penny stock companies. They rarely, if ever, make the front pages. All this makes it very risky to trade in penny stocks. On the flip side, however, the rewards can be fantastic. Let us examine why the shares of such companies are considered as high-risk.

They are high-risk shares because of the following factors:

- Low volume
- Low market capitalization
- High volatility

- Very little regulation

- Susceptible to manipulation

- Not listed on major stock exchanges

- Very little history or information available

- Low liquidity

One of the most important aspects to bear in mind is that you need information for making sound choices about buying and selling stocks. Any trader who rushes in blindfolded is a fool. This is precisely what happens if you trade penny stocks without an iota of information. When it comes to trading stocks, information is gold. Have you noticed graphs and charts about penny stock companies? Probably not. This is because large-cap companies have enough information publicly available but not penny stock companies. Even if you dig hard, such information may not be available for penny stock companies. Very little information, if at all, is available about the company and its performance. This makes it impossible to make proper decisions, as one can never be certain of anything regarding the company and its shares. In the absence of such vitally important information, you will most likely make poor choices.

Another important aspect is 'market cap' or market capitalization. These companies often have very low market capitalization. This also means that liquidity is often very low. In other words, sellers may not always be able to sell their shares if the volume of shares being sold goes up significantly. Consequently, they may be forced to sell at a much lower price and hence suffer a significant loss. Most traders love high volumes as this allows people to buy and sell quickly. The ability to close a deal quickly is significantly higher when the volume of shares being traded is higher. Perhaps the most important reason for wariness among traders is that fact there is very little regulation when it comes to penny stocks. Since these penny stocks are not listed on the major stock exchanges, these companies need not disclose a lot of information. In fact, they divulge very little about the company performance and what is expected in the near future.

Understanding the Risks

Now let us try and put things in proper perspective and understand the risks posed by trading in penny stocks. There are quite a few risks such as:

- Lack of company related information
- No history of trades available
- Open to manipulation
- Price volatility
- Volume volatility
- Misinformation and rumormongering
- Lack of liquidity
- Now let us understand each risk separately.
- Lack of Company-Related Information

Most of the penny stock companies are very small companies and not much information is available about them. The size of the company, the number of employees, and the capital invested, are all-important to understand. However, none of this is available. All this makes it impossible to decide on the future prospects of a company.

No History of Trades

What about trading history? Not your own trading history, but a history of the performance of the company shares. This can be of vital significance when it comes to making a decision about the company shares. The performance of a company can be judged by the way the shares have been performing over a period of time. Sadly, this information is absent for penny stock companies.

Open to Manipulation

Shares of penny stock companies are extremely susceptible to manipulation. It is easy to manipulate shares of company that trade at low prices and at low volumes. If you have sufficient funds, you can manipulate the price movements. This is precisely what big players can do. Imagine what banks and financial institutions can do with their huge portfolios. Banks have millions of dollars to play with and they can manipulate the markets. They can even manipulate the price movements of large-cap companies. Imagine what they can do with micro-cap companies and small-cap companies.

Price Volatility

Price movements can be pretty rapid when it comes to stocks. This is more so in the case of penny stocks. So, when there is price volatility, you could be vulnerable. A rapid movement in prices can wipe you out even before you realize it. Hence, you have to be mindful of price volatility.

Volume Volatility

This is where it can get really tricky. Volume volatility means the number of shares being traded at any given time is very high. Now, while this may be a good thing, one has to be very watchful. High volume makes you vulnerable as the prices are always matched to volume volatility. The higher the volume volatility, the higher the price volatility. You could see a runaway price change in the wrong direction. This could wipe your trade out in minutes. Hence, this poses a very high risk to you as well.

Misinformation and Rumor-mongering

This is possibly the least understood risk factor. People do not realize it but these days it is easy to spread rumors. The Internet is the perfect medium to spread a rumor. It is a tool that can allow unscrupulous people to speared misinformation quickly. This is a risk factor because people and traders who spread rumors about penny stocks stand to gain by spreading misinformation. Such unscrupulous traders influence the movement of prices in order to drive the prices in their desired direction. You could fall prey easily to such rumormongering. You have to watch out for this.

Lack of Liquidity

Lack of liquidity means the lack of money being exchanged between buyers and sellers of shares. This might mean that you may not have enough buyers to trade with when you decide to sell your stocks. This in turn could mean that you would have to wait until someone is prepared to buy your shares. This could take a long time. Meanwhile, the prices could continue to drop. Finally, when you do get a buyer, it may be too late and you may end up with a loss. This is something you want to avoid. Hence, liquidity or rather the lack of liquidity could be a major risk factor.

CHAPTER SIX

Ensuring A Positive Return

As with all stocks, it is all about timing. If you get the timing right, you come away smiling and happy. If you get it wrong, then even indulging in a huge beerfest will not help you get over it. Hence, with penny stocks it is all about buying when you believe there is a good chance of the price climbing even further. You buy when it is low and sell when it is high enough. But how do you judge when the price is just right to buy or when it is right enough to sell? This is the million-dollar question. What are the indicators that you should be looking at?

Consider the following at any given time:

- **Volume of shares being traded**
- **Volatility**
- **Liquidity**
- **Recent history**

When you see that the volume of shares being traded is low, it is a warning sign. It would be far better for you to wait for volume to pick up. Why is this necessary? This is because, when volume is low, you have a lower chance of selling back the stock. You may be forced to wait for a long time. This may force down the prices. You could lose all the profits and even incur a loss.

Volatility refers to the fluctuation in prices and is the result of quick buying and selling. Volatility is often the result of high volumes. Hence, the higher the volatility the better it is to buy penny stocks. Now why is this so important? This is significant as high volatility permits you to wait longer for the price to hit the expected levels. This means you have a greater chance of selling the stock at a much higher price.

Volume of shares being traded, volatility, and liquidity are all inter-related. Liquidity refers to the amount of money available for buying and selling penny stocks. When volume is low, volatility is usually low and so is liquidity. When liquidity is low, there may not be enough money to go around. In other words, there may not be enough money for your penny stocks to be sold at a higher price. Another aspect to bear in mind is when to sell once you have registered a profit. How much time should you wait before pressing the sell button? Should you sell now or wait for the price to rise further? Should you book your profits now? The ideal way to go around this is to wait until you have about 30% profit. In other words, wait till you have a 30% increase in share price before you sell. Now why is this so? This is because of the nature of penny stocks. You must never forget that these are penny stocks. They are also referred to as micro-cap stocks. This means you are not likely to see a great rise in prices.

So why take chances! It is more than likely that the trend will reverse once you have about 30% to 40% profits. Let us take an example. Suppose you buy, a thousand shares of a company X at $0.50 and then wait for the share price to rise. Your investment is $500 and you are looking for 30% profit. Now when the price hits $0.65, you hit the sell button. You make $650 and your profit is a reasonable $150. Now this is not a bad deal! You have made a 30% return on your investment.

The problem starts when you believe that the price will continue to rise and go past this dollar mark. These are penny stocks and this usually does not happen. It is far better to be safe than sorry. For most investors the need to make money is the key motivator. However, this can work against you. If you simply "have to make money" then you are in trouble. This need to "make money at all cost" gets investors into trouble. This causes them to act irresponsibly and make unsound decisions based on their urgent need to make money. What you need to understand is that the market has a mind of its own. Sometimes, more of than not, the market goes against the expected norm. This is when you simply cannot afford to lose your cool. You have to have the courage to stay the course despite everything. If you have the patience, you will be rewarded. This is how you make money with penny stocks.

Another important aspect is the timing, when you buy and when you sell. This can play a pivotal role in your success or failure as a penny stock trader. This is where prior knowledge and the latest information can make a huge difference. It is vital to stay updated in the trading game. Make sure you have taken the trouble to garner every bit of information you can. There are financial blogs and websites that provide the latest figures and economic data. Never miss out on this. You can subscribe to newsletters from reputable financial blogs and magazines to stay current and updated.

Staying Focused

The key to a wining trade is always about staying focused. Prepare for a trade just as you would prepare for an important interview. Do not trade if there is no opportunity. Watch and wait for the right moment. Remember, patience is the watchword.

Don't Get Too Greedy

Greed is the root of all that is evil, so the saying goes. Well, this could not be truer than in the case of penny stock trading. Greed could destroy a winning trade. You must have a profit figure in mind and then when you reach it, you must press the sell button. Many traders have thrown away a potentially winning trade all because of greed. The golden rule is, there is always another trade waiting for you.

Wait for Volumes to Hit Highs

You must wait for volumes of a given stock to reach a certain level. Once you observe that a certain stock is trading with high volume and the price is just right, press the buy button. This means there is a good chance that prices will continue to rise. As the volume is high, you will find buyers very quickly when you decide to sell. This is the key to success. Neglect this rule at your peril.

Minimize Your Risks

Now this may appear simple, but I assure you it is the least understood aspect of trading. Some traders simply do not get it. You are there to make money and not lose it. If you are very keen on losing your hard-earned cash, why not give it away to charity. Remember, ***MINIMIZE YOUR RISKS***. Now how can you minimize your risks? Here are a few things to consider when you want to minimize your risks:

- **Use low leverage**
- **Use less than 2% of available trading capital**
- **Set predetermined loss/profit levels**

One of the craziest things you can do is to use high leverage. Now, leverage is something that many traders simply do not understand. In an effort to make money quickly, the tendency on the part of most traders is to use high leverage. Every trading platform allows traders to use leverage. High leverage means you are the broker is allowing you to maximize your profits but at the same time, you also maximize your risks. This is often not understood. When you use low leverage, you actually lower your chances of suffering a losing trade. You may make small profits but you definitely won't lose money. Using a small percentage of trading capital on every trade is another important aspect to keep in mind. Nothing is certain in the world of penny stocks. So, why take chances. You must use approximately 2% or less of available funds on a given trade. This way you will not stand to lose all your money on a single trade.

Let us say you have $5000 in your trading account. Now, it would be silly to start a trade with $5000 or even $2000. Instead, it would be better to start a trade with $ 100. Yes, your profits would be less, but you will lose at the most $100. Live today, trade another day – this should be your motto. Now comes the hard part. No matter what happens, stick to your trade. Remember, plan your trade and do not trade your plan. Even if things go against you, stick it out and be patient. This strategy will make you less anxious and apprehensive. You will be a better penny stock trader as a result of this strategy. Wait for your trade to reach the predetermined profit levels. Once you have reached your target price, you can collect your profits.

Self-Discipline

Who has not heard the old adage that says it takes self-discipline to achieve success in any field? The same applies to trading in penny stocks. It will take time to establish that cast iron self-discipline to trade stocks. You will need to learn a lot and control that urge to hit the sell/buy button. Self-discipline will transform you from a panicky and jumpy nervous trader to a bold and decisive trader. Self-discipline will take you through turbulent times and you will emerge a more determined and savvy trader.

If you use these strategies time after time, you will become a master penny stock trader. It takes patience and skill to become a penny stock trader and this are the best strategies you could execute.

CHAPTER SEVEN
Specific Trading Strategies

Stock trading, specifically penny stock trading, requires a well researched and developed strategy. People who fail to make money with penny stocks often blame their luck, when in reality, it is not luck but strategy, will to succeed, and discipline that determine success in penny stock investing.

All successful stock traders have a strategy that they have developed before they enter the market that they strictly follow and very rarely deviate from, regardless of day-to-day market fluctuations. The development of this strategy is a process and it requires hard work and research, however, it is undeniably what separates consistent winners from consistent losers. Understanding the importance of having a strategy, now you must learn how to develop one that works for you. In order to maximize your success in penny stock trading you must have a specific strategy for each position you have, meaning each stock you purchase. You should know each of these strategies in and out and be fully capable of explaining to a complete novice who knows absolutely nothing about the stock market why you have chosen to invest in that specific stock.

While developing your strategy for penny stock investing you must follow these sacred rules of investing which are applicable regardless of what type of stock you are purchasing:

- Do not believe everything you read about a stock, rather, take into consideration information from many sources and make an educated decision based on ALL of the information that you have available to you

- Never act on a tip unless you do your own research on the stock first. As Jim Cramer says, "tips are for waiters." Never blindly follow the tip of someone unless you fully understand the stock and have done your own research!

- Learn to avoid rumors. Again, never act on a rumor you have heard about a stock. Always do your homework and create your own justification for your position.

- Be prepared to sell quickly. Don't wait around and try to "ride it out." When your research points to an upcoming decline in the share price of your stock or a current decline, cut your losses and get out of that position!

Again, you should develop a specific strategy for every position you have. First, collect and document the following information for the stock.

- **Trade history**

- Price history
- Recent price changes/movement/volatility
- Company performance
- Company background
- Market conditions

All these factors will assist you in forming your comprehensive trading strategy for the stock. You must study and fully understand the above factors carefully before forming a strategy. Now lets take a specific example. Let us suppose Bob is a penny stock trader. Bob is desperate to make money with penny stocks. Nevertheless, Bob must first formulate a strategy before purchasing ANY penny stocks. He calls his buddy Jake and asks him what he has heard about the current penny stocks on the market. Jake is an ill informed investor and passes on some of what he has heard to Bob. Bob should buy 'stock X' as it is at its lowest and it is expected to rise by 5% in the next five trading days! Now, Bob is a novice at this game and relies on Jake heavily. He invests $10,000 in 'stock X' at $1.45 and waits for it to climb. Guess what! Surprise! Surprise! His chosen stock plummets even further. He is at a complete loss to explain the events that lead to this financial disaster. What's even worse is that Bob does not quit and refuses to pull out of the stock and cut his losses, believing that his luck is going to turn around eventually. Oh yes, it does turn around, but only after Bob's stop loss point has been reached. Bob gets wiped out. End of story: a sad story that could have been avoided easily.

So, what went wrong and why? What was it that Bob failed to do? Bob failed to do the most fundamental part of penny stock investing, the first step! He failed to study the price history and recent price movements of 'stock X', he failed do his own homework and develop his own strategy.   He acted on a 'tip' from someone and did not do his own research on the stock before purchasing.   Had he done even a little research, he would have realized that this stock had yet a long way to go down before steadily climbing back up yet again. A simple check into the price movement of the stock could have saved his neck (and his wallet of course). This is the first lesson you need to learn when making your specific trading strategy while trading penny stocks. The second lesson concerns the immediate price movements. This will allow you to fix an entry point. Your entry and exit from a stock must be perfectly timed. In the case of the above example with Bob, his entry and exit timing was quite poor. Had he entered the trade a little later and subsequently exited when the share price increased, he would have made a handsome profit.

You must check the most recent price movement and then enter a trade to maximize your profits. Never forget this maxim: ***Know The Company!*** At the end of the day, you are trading shares of a company. People very often forget to do research on the company when purchasing a stock, rather focusing strictly on the stock itself. You must also know everything you can about the company whose stock you are purchasing. Sure, understanding the numbers side of the game and having all the information on the stock is important, but possibly even more critical is knowing about the actual company, their mission, their target market, their executives, their history, who is funding them etc. Ask yourself: What is the market-cap of company 'X'? Does it have a poor history of performance? How have the markets responded to company 'X'? Is there any scandal or bad financial news concerning the company? Are there any plans in the pipeline for company 'X'? Who is the CEO of company 'X'? Where else has he/she worked before? How did those companies perform? A little research will lead you to the answers that you seek. It is your diligence in finding out all about company 'X' that will pay rich dividends in the end! Had Bob bothered to do his research, he would have found out that company 'X' had no plans for expansion and that there were rumors of bankruptcy.

Some of this may appear trivial at first but remember; it is your money that is on the line. Should you disregard any scrap of information that has the potential to affect your financial future? You must take every piece of information you can find, into consideration when creating your strategy for penny stock investing regardless how important it might seem. This is how Bob should have developed his specific trading strategy for his chosen penny stock. Bob should have:

- **Studied the history of company 'X'. The Internet is his friend when it comes to doing a little company research. Almost anything you need to know regarding up and coming companies can be found in news articles across the Internet.**

Ensure to not only read one, but many different articles!

- Made a brief note of recent price movements of the stock.

- Reviewed the historical highs/lows prices of the stock.

- Try to determine the best entry point after careful evaluation of the price movements of the day.

- Look for any news events relating to the company 'X'.

- Look for any economic data released by the company in recent times.

All this would have made Bob aware of what was going on with respect to the prices of 'Stock X'. He would have been more careful when initiating a trade with the above-mentioned 'stock X'. Had he done this, he would have probably waited for the prices to move lower and then initiated a trade with a smaller amount.

If you are prepared to do your homework and be patient for your entry point to be reached, you have a fairly good chance of being on the profitable end of a penny stock trade. It is impossible to develop a penny stock trading strategy that would be applicable to all penny stocks and to all investors. Each investor should use the information that is available to them to create a strategy that will allow them to reach their specific goals for that position.

CHAPTER EIGHT

Recent Penny Stock Trading Examples

Now let us take a close look at some concrete examples of good penny stock trades and bad penny stock trades. You must remember that all bad trades are the result of bad planning. If you research and plan your trades carefully, there is no reason why you cannot succeed with penny stock trading.

Here are some examples of penny stocks that went through the roof and really mad people some money. Most of them started well below $5.00 and therefore were once considered penny stocks. Some were even valued at less than a dollar per share when they were first listed on the pink sheets! Take a look at some of the penny stocks listed in the examples below and their price per share differences. It makes for very interesting reading that is at the same time quite inspiring. Note the lowest price of the penny stock and also the current price of the stock.

Inhibitex:	$2.35	-	$24.08
Cellstar:	$1.44	-	$13.50

Iomega:	$3.25	- $13.90
Nanophase:	$3.75	- $16.75
Immunomedics:	$1.44	- $29.12
Total Renal Care:	$3.12	- $26.95
Voxware:	$ 0.90	- $10.31
Corvas:	$3.00	- $23.25
Cytogen:	$2.12	- $17.50
Verilink:	$3.00	- $14.62
GeneLabs:	$2.31	- $10.72

Lets us take the case of Voxware. This was a penny stock company that made several investors a large sum of money. In the early life of the company, shares were trading at .90 cents. Yes, that is right. 90 cents a share! Now look at the maximum share price that the stock reached, $10.31. If you would have timed your entry and exit points for this stock perfectly and had invested, say $1,000 in Voxware then imagine your profits. Take a look: *$1,000/.90 = about 1,112 shares.* You would have bought *1112 shares* and your investment would be *$1,000.* Then at *$10.31 a share*, these shares would have been worth: *$10.31 X 1112 = $11,464.* What a fantastic return on your investment! Would you not love to be in this situation? All of us would. Let us look another one of the former penny stocks listed above.

Take the case of Cellstar. The stock was at *$1.44* in its early stages. At its high point, the stocks traded at *$13.50*. Again, let us say you have bought *1,000 shares* when the price was a dollar exactly. Your investment would be: *$1.00 X 1000 shares = $1,000*. Now you decide to sell the shares when the price reached *$11.00*. Now let us calculate your profits and your rate of return. *$11 X 1000 shares = $11,000*. So, your profit would be: *$11,000 – $1000 = $10,000*. Hence, your rate of return on your investment would be: 10000/1000 X 100 = *1000% (thousand percent)*. As you can see the rate of return on your investment would be a staggering thousand percent. That is penny stocks for you.

There is also, however, the other side of penny stocks. The ugly side of penny stocks is that you could end up losing a lot of money when things go wrong. What about those investors who had bought Nanophase when the shares stood at about $16.50? This would have been a disaster. Let us take a look at another fictitious trade as an example of a bad trade.

Let us say you have just bought thousand shares of Nanophase at $16.50. Your investment would be: $16.50 X 1000 shares = $16,500. Now you wait patiently for the shares to rise, unfortunately, the prices plummet instead. They fall and keep falling. Now, you are faced with two choices; sell your shares as quickly as you can and cut your losses or wait for the trend to reverse and for the prices to rise again. Panic hits you and you begin to sweat as you see your loses begin to pile up.

Finally, it gets too much for you and you hit the sell button. Wham! You get hit with a terrible loss as you sell at $ 10 per share. On selling, you get back: $10 X 1,000 shares = 10,000. Your loss would be: $16,500 – $10,000 = $6,500. Your loss percent would be: 6500/16500 X 100 =

39.39 or almost 40% loss. Actually, you are lucky you got away with a loss of only 40%. It could have been far worse.

This is what trading penny stock trading is all about. You need to watch your step. There is a great deal of apprehension about penny stock trading and this is more due to misinformation and rumor mongering. People read about how dangerous it is to trade penny stocks and decide to never do enough research in trade properly. Those who have had the courage to follow their heart have made it big with penny stocks. After all, not much can be achieved in life without taking a few risks.

CONCLUSION

If you are just beginning your journey in investing, or a seasoned veteran, I hope this book was able to shed some light on the world of penny stocks. I am confident that the combination of the knowledge and strategies presented in this book along with the determination and drive to succeed; anyone will be able to cash in on Penny Stocks.

The next step is to put these strategies into action. It is time for you to test your newly acquired knowledge with penny stocks and give the stock market all you have. Remember that knowledge without action will amount to nothing. It is only when the two are combined will success be achieved. I really want to thank you for reading this book and I sincerely hope that you received value from it.

Thank you and good luck!

ABOUT
CLYDEBANK FINANCE

ClydeBank Finance is a division of the multimedia publishing firm ClydeBank Media LLC. ClydeBank Media's goal is to provide affordable, accessible information to a global market through different forms of media such as eBooks, paperback books and audio books. Company divisions are based on subject matter, each consisting of a dedicated team of researchers, writers, editors and designers. The Finance division of ClydeBank Media is composed of contributors who are experts in their given disciplines. Contributors originate from diverse areas of the world to guarantee the presented information fosters a global perspective.

Contributors have multiple years of experience in personal finance, budgeting, money management, wealth management, investing and many other areas of discipline.

For more information, please visit us at :

www.clydebankmedia.com

or contact us at :

info@clydebankmedia.com

PREVIEW OF

Bitcoin Beginner's Guide :
Everything You Need To Know To Get Rich With Bitcoins

Chapter 1 : What Are Bitcoins?

Imagine a way wherein you could anonymously transfer money to anyone instantly, anywhere in the world. Someone is selling something that you want to buy, and you don't want the hassle of transferring funds from a bank account or credit card, or exchanging dollars for pounds or yens – you just want to make an easy and permanent transaction.

If you happen to have a virtual wallet full of bitcoins you are in luck! Especially if those bitcoins are more valuable now than they were when you obtained them, giving you more buying power or simply the ability to trade them for a nice sum of cash. Before we get into the nuts and bolts of how to actually make money with this unique form of currency, you will need an understanding of what bitcoins are and how they are used. You need to know what it is that makes this anonymous currency so valuable and why people are motivated to use it for various transactions in place of many of the various world currencies in circulation.

So what exactly are bitcoins? Bitcoin is a decentralized, peer-to-peer, virtual currency that was created by a web developer who call himself Satoshi Nakamoto. I say this because Satoshi Nakamoto is widely thought to be only a pseudonym for the mysterious inventor. We'll review the history of Bitcoin in the next chapter so we're not going to discuss much of it here. But in order to understand the nature of this online currency, it is important to know who invented bitcoin and why. Bitcoin is the system that Nakamoto invented and bitcoin is the actual unit of this virtual currency.

The concept of virtual currency has been around almost as long as the internet, providing users a means of exchanging goods and services for currency virtually instantly, without government regulation and with the ability of conducting transactions over great distances and across borders without having to exchange different currencies.

Previous forms of virtual currency had some significant problems, one being that they could be duplicated without value, and there was no real way to verify transactions. For example, one could have an account full of what we'll call "e-bucks" with which one could purchase some goods or services online. However, once the transaction was in process, there was no third party to ensure that the transaction actually took place and actually transferred some intrinsic value from one account to the next. The value of an e-buck literally was based on whatever the holder of the currency or buyer said it was, and what the seller thought it was. There was no way to prevent someone from creating an account full of e-bucks that had no real value. The e-buck was essentially an IOU that could be priceless or worthless depending on the integrity of the issuer of the IOU itself. Let's say I trade an IOU consisting of 10 e-bucks to you for a trinket, and you take those same e-bucks and try to trade them to Joe for one of his trinkets. Joe could question the value of your e-bucks because they came from me and he doesn't know me. Then you could come back to me and demand your trinket back because the e-bucks I gave you are not valuable to Joe. For that matter, let's say that I originally purchased the e-bucks I gave you from an online source for 100 US dollars with my credit card. I could demand that the credit card issuer reverse the original transaction because the e-bucks I bought were no good. The value of any non-commodity backed currency depends upon a consensus of the users on its value; that is, people must agree on what the currency is worth. You can see how complex and ridiculous this can get! Nakamoto developed a system that did not suffer from these problems (though the success of bitcoin does still require a consensus). Bitcoin transactions are permanent, irreversible, and somewhat anonymous, helping to make them such an attractive form of currency!

Similar to gold, silver, or other types of commodity-backed currency, Bitcoin has a value that is based on supply and demand. And like gold, the supply of bitcoins is provided by only two sources: people who already have them and people who mine them. That's right, bitcoins are actually mined, and there is a limited supply to be mined. The effort that goes into mining them and the fact that there is a limited supply are both factors that contribute to the value of bitcoin. As of the date of this writing, there are around 12 million bitcoins in existence with a block of 25 new bitcoins being mined every 10 minutes or so. As the number of bitcoin increases, that is every 210,000 blocks of bitcoin, the number created by mining them is reduced by half. At the current rate of mining, bitcoin should top out at around 21 million in 125 years or so.

Chapter 2 : Where Did Bitcoins Come From and Why?

As we've briefly discussed in Chapter 1, the internet seemed to be ripe for the concept of digital or virtual currency almost from day one. Prior to Bitcoin, none of the virtual currencies seemed to last long. A group of dedicated internet users called cryptographers, those concerned with developing secure methods of making transactions over the internet in the presence of third parties, dedicated themselves to developing a strong virtual currency as early as the 1990's.

One attempt at such an anonymous currency system was made by a man named David Chaum. His currency, called ecash, relied on government and credit card company infrastructures that were already in place when he developed the system in the early 1990's. This made ecash subject to manipulation and instability that contributed to its eventual failure. Another virtual currency emerged in the 1990's that was called DigiCash. While initially successful due to its anonymity, it eventually failed in 1998 due to partnerships with banks that disallowed the anonymity. A system called CyberCash came onto the scene in 1994, and actually went public with a $300-million stock offering. Also attractive to users due to offered anonymity, CyberCash was initially successful but eventually filed for bankruptcy in 2001 after technical glitches that included Y2K bugs.

Meanwhile, a currency called Flooz was short lived due to its failure to provide secure transactions, including the problem of double spending. Another form of virtual currency includes those that are accumulated and spent in the virtual world such as World of Warcraft, Second Life, and Facebook. These virtual world currencies seem to fulfill their intended purpose but have little use outside of gaming. There are and have been others, but none as versatile as Bitcoin.

Satoshi Nakamoto published his paper in 2008 in which he detailed a new type of virtual currency that solved one problem previous forms of virtual currency had – the problem of double spending. As we mentioned in Chapter 1, Bitcoin is not the first form of digital currency devised, but may be proven to be more successful than its predecessors. One of the reasons for this is that bitcoin is not subject to double spending; that is, once a person has spent a bitcoin, it is gone and that person no longer has access to it. Each bitcoin is unique with its own serial number; bitcoins cannot be duplicated or copied and transactions are completely irreversible. Nakamoto used a system of decentralized computers that could verify each transaction and eliminate the double spending problem. In fact, it is the process of verifying transactions that bitcoin miners perform that adds value to the system and creates new blocks of bitcoins.

The domain name Bitcoin.org was registered in 2008 and the first batch of bitcoins were issued in 2009, presumably to Nakamoto when he mined the first block of 50 bitcoins. When bitcoins were first traded they were valued at a rate of $0.0003 per 1,000 bitcoins! The first known bitcoin transaction did not take place until 2010 when a Florida computer programmer by the name of Laszlo Hanyecz used them to purchase two pizzas for the handsome sum of 10,000 bitcoins. The year 2010 also saw the establishment of Mt. Gox, the first Bitcoin exchange, which gave users a marketplace for trading with and storing bitcoins. That first year of trading ended with the bitcoin valued at $0.30 each.

In 2011, Bitcoin became more widely known and sought after following an article by Andy Greenberg. That article, published in Forbes Magazine, described some of the attributes of the virtual currency. Subsequently, Bitcoin's popularity and value soared. Many of the system users that had spent spare time verifying transactions for bitcoin had mined and collected bitcoins that became tremendously valuable. People began to invest in bitcoins out of speculation, and groups of bitcoin miners began to mine bitcoins with the sole purpose of making money by selling mined bitcoins. By late 2013, Bitcoin had been valued at over US$1,000 each, presumably making many of the previous Bitcoin owners a great deal of money; this happened despite the fairly volatile US Dollar value of bitcoin throughout that year, fluctuating by hundreds of dollars due to speculation and publicity. In late 2013, the US Federal Bureau of Investigation shut down one popular "Deep Web" website called Silk Road, which was used to conduct illicit transactions such as the buying and selling of illegal drugs using bitcoins. The website later came back online, calling itself Silk Road 2.0, and resumed doing business as before.

In January of 2014, the total number of transaction blocks reached 210,000, and the bitcoin reward for mining halved from 50 bitcoins to 25 bitcoins. Bitcoin reward for mining will remain at 25 for 4 years; that is until 2017, when it will halve again to 12.5 bitcoins. Four years later, it will be reduced to 6.25 bitcoins, and so on. This process is automated by the software that Nakamoto devised and thus fixes the maximum amount of bitcoins that can be generated. The Bitcoin software essentially calculates the rate of bitcoin production after each 2,016 transactions, and adjusts the difficulty of the problem solving involved in authenticating transactions to keep the rate of new bitcoin production (mining) steady for around 4 years. We will discuss the process of mining further in Chapter 3, but the process utilizes voluntary computing power and proof of work concepts to authenticate and permanently record transactions that occur between users.

As of the date of this writing, Bitcoin's future seems uncertain, with the possibility of government regulation threatening to scare off users and investors. Two of the most trafficked Bitcoin exchanges, Mt.

Gox and Bitstamp temporarily halted trading in early 2014 to work out a flaw in the public transaction ledger system that seemed to allow some users to attempt to hide, fake, or even duplicate transactions. While the potential threat made some new and prospective bitcoin users nervous, experienced users remained unfazed and bullish about the future of Bitcoin. However, as is true with many uncertain and volatile investments, bitcoin could prove to be an incredible money maker for those willing to do their proverbial homework and assume a certain level of risk.

Made in the USA
Lexington, KY
15 October 2015